William Carlos Williams

William Carlos Williams. *Photograph by John D. Schiff*

William Carlos Williams

Papers by

Kenneth Burke
Emily Mitchell Wallace
Norman Holmes Pearson
A. M. Sullivan

Edited by Charles Angoff

Rutherford • *Madison* • *Teaneck*
FAIRLEIGH DICKINSON UNIVERSITY PRESS
London: ASSOCIATED UNIVERSITY PRESSES

Associated University Presses, Inc.
Cranbury, New Jersey 08512

Associated University Presses
108 New Bond Street
London W1Y OQX, England

Emily Mitchell Wallace wishes to thank Mrs. William Carlos Williams and New Directions Publishing Corporation for permission to use quotations from the following: *The Collected Earlier Poems,* copyright 1938, 1951 by William Carlos Williams; *Paterson, Book One,* copyright 1946 by William Carlos Williams; *The Autobiography of William Carlos Williams,* copyright 1951 by William Carlos Williams; *Selected Essays,* copyright 1954 by William Carlos Williams; *Journey to Love,* copyright © 1955 by William Carlos Williams; *Imaginations,* copyright © 1970 by Florence H. Williams. Quotations from unpublished letters, the parody "Trees," and the holograph of "Tree," all by William Carlos Williams, copyright © 1974 by Florence H. Williams.

Acknowledgment is also made to Yale University Library for permission to reproduce the holograph of "Tree," and to Lockwood Memorial Library, State University of New York at Buffalo, for "Trees."

She is grateful also for permission to use quotations from unpublished essays by William Eric Williams, copyright © 1974 by William Eric Williams.

Library of Congress Cataloging in Publication Data
Main entry under title:
William Carlos Williams.
    (Leverton lecture series)
    From a program held at the Rutherford campus on Nov. 12, 1972.
    1. Williams, William Carlos, 1883–1963.
I. Burke, Kenneth, 1897–   II. Angoff, Charles, 1902–
ed. III. Series.
PS3545.I544Z96   811'.5'2   73-10757
ISBN 0-8386-1441-8

Contents

Foreword

This is the first in the projected group of publications to be known as the Leverton Lecture Series. The lectures are made possible by the generosity of Dr. Morris Leverton, a retired financier and a member of the Board of Overseers of Fairleigh Dickinson University.

Each of the three main campuses is having its own Leverton Lectures. The Leverton Lectures of the Rutherford Campus are emphasizing the contributions of New Jersey to the national culture in various areas—literary, musical, scientific, religious, philosophical, political. We hope that by 1976, the bicentenary, our Leverton Lectures, and other events, altogether, will show what an important part New Jersey has played in virtually all aspects of the national life. The first such lecture took place in Rutherford on November 12, 1972. It dealt with the career and poetical achievements of Dr. William Carlos Williams, the pediatrician-cum-poet who spent his most productive years in Rutherford. He was a sort of patron saint of Fairleigh Dickinson University.

]7[

Three authorities on the writings of Dr. Williams presented papers, each of which made a contribution to the mounting body of research and interpretation concerning Dr. Williams. These papers are reproduced herein. There were other features, such as a portrait from memory, so to speak, of William Carlos Williams, also included here, by the eminent poet, critic, and authority on New Jersey literary culture, A. M. Sullivan, who is a former president of The Poetry Society of America. The entire program of the first Symposium follows.

Dr. Charles Angoff
Chairman,
Leverton Fund Committee
Fairleigh Dickinson University
Rutherford Campus
Rutherford, New Jersey

The Program

INTRODUCTORY REMARKS
  Dr. Charles Angoff, Professor Emeritus of English, Fairleigh Dickinson University
WELCOME
  Dr. J. Osborn Fuller, President, Fairleigh Dickinson University
IN THE AMERICAN GRAIN
  A film featuring E. G. Marshall and William Carlos Williams
A CRITICAL APPRECIATION
  Kenneth Burke
HUNTING DOWN THE POEMS (retitled "The Forms of the Emotions . . . the Pointed Trees")
  Emily Mitchell Wallace
THE PEOPLE WHO USE THE
WILLIAM CARLOS WILLIAMS COLLECTION
AT YALE
  Norman Holmes Pearson

THE VOICE OF WILLIAM CARLOS WILLIAMS
Selections from an actual recording of the poet reading his own works

REVERIE AND INVOCATION
The Fairleigh Dickinson University Chamber Choir, under the direction of Louis Hooker, performing a Williams poem set to music by Stanley Purdy.

READINGS
from Williams's poetry by David Ross

The Participants

A prolific writer and lecturer, critic KENNETH BURKE has received numerous awards and six honorary degrees. At the time of this Memorial he had recently returned from conferences on communications in Barcelona, and was giving a seminar on "Mimesis" at Wesleyan College.

LOUIS HOOKER, founder, music director, and principal conductor of the New Jersey Schola Cantorum, teaches voice and choral conducting at the Rutherford Campus of Fairleigh Dickinson University as Associate Professor of Music.

NORMAN PEARSON holds degrees from the University of Berlin, of Oxford, and Yale University. He currently holds a professorship at Yale in English and American studies. An expert on American literature, he has numerous scholarly publications to his credit.

A graduate of Bucknell University and New York University, STANLEY PURDY is Associate Professor and Chairman of the Department of Fine Arts at Fairleigh

Dickinson University's Rutherford Campus. A composer of jazz and contemporary serious music, his works include motion picture scores, ballet, and symphonic and vocal compositions.

DAVID ROSS was one of the first broadcasters to introduce the reading of good poetry on the air. His memorable program "Poet's Gold" is just one of his accomplishments; he has won several prizes for his own works from the Poetry Society of America and has given readings in colleges, study groups, and the Library of Congress.

EMILY MITCHELL WALLACE has taught English, creative writing and American literature at the University of Pennsylvania and Swarthmore College. She has published the definitive bibliography of William Carlos Williams's published writing and is working on a new edition of Williams's letters.

William Carlos Williams

William Carlos Williams. *Photograph by Charles Sheeler*

William Carlos Williams:
A Critical Appreciation

KENNETH BURKE

Let us have, for our text, this poem from *Spring And All:*

In passing with my mind
on nothing in the world
but the right of way
I enjoy on the road by
virtue of the law—
I saw
an elderly man who
smiled and looked away
to the north past a house—
a woman in blue
who was laughing and
leaning forward to look up
into the man's half
averted face
and a boy of eight who was
looking at the middle of

the man's belly
at a watchchain—
The supreme importance
of this nameless spectacle
sped me by them
without a word—
Why bother where I went?
for I went spinning on the
four wheels of my car
along the wet road until
I saw a girl with one leg
over the rail of a balcony

When rereading some of the early material that is re-
published in the volume *Imaginations,* edited by Webster
Schott, I got to thinking: To what extent might this poetry
be, as it were, the very essence of traffic? The poem I have
quoted is explicitly of this sort, on traffic as seen in multi-
farious irregularities, or as a constant succession of momen-
tary fragments, which we experience in disrelated bits as
sharp as snapshots.

There it is, unmistakably. But I also had in mind, first of
all, a similar bubbling up, wholly from within, an outpour-
ing of what has more the quality of dissociations than of
associations. The improvisings in this regard produce an
effect almost the opposite of what I feel when following
the *Ideenflucht,* line by line, in the poetry of Conrad Aiken.

This mode of incessant, ebullient *leaping* from word to
word (one could hardly even say "from sentence to sentence") gets summed up, in the original introduction to
Kora in Hell, thus:

> I thought at first to adjoin to each improvisation a more or less
> opaque commentary. But the mechanical interference that would
> result makes this inadvisable. Instead I have placed some of them
> in the preface where without losing their original intention . . .
> they relieve the later text and also add their weight to my present
> fragmentary argument.

]16[

I was enchanted with the possibilities of the form as I saw it; namely, a set of *free* associations (or dissociations) which, in each case, would be tied down by translation into a kind of "argument," preferably less rather than more opaque, summing up in somewhat pedestrian fashion, as with Dante in his *Vita Nuova,* the gist of the particular motive or motif in which the given improvisation had been centrifugally grounded.

But Dante's world was a time of pilgrimage. Here, I felt, we had a world of traffic, particularly inasmuch as, already in those early days of *Contact,* New Jersey had begun to confront its destiny as a kind of "Vestibule" State, which the nation tramples over, on its way to or from New York. Particularly is this so of the area where William Carlos Williams lived—and he, of all poets, was most sensitive to the motivating conditions of his region.

In an article on Marianne Moore (1932, reprinted in *The William Carlos Williams Reader*) Williams tells us that a poem of hers is to be viewed as "an anthology of transit." There, in his role as critic, he finds it "thrilling" that, while occupying a thought "to its end," she "goes on— without connectives." And the idea is repeated in a reference to her procedure "without connectives unless it be poetry, the inevitable connective, if you will." In such appreciations, it seems to me, the writer is talking about a poetic motive that comes close to characterizing the source of his own copiousness. But for him I would replace "transit" with "traffic." And behind this thought would be the general notion that the copiousness of the poet's imagination was linked with a sense of fragmentary, dissociated vignettes, welling from within, as the glancingly, yet minutely observed details of the Williams poem I quoted were encountered from without.

In contrast with that poem, one might think of Dante's

]17[

progress through the various circles in the *Divine Comedy* (a work also characterized by a series of bits encountered en route, as a few details are imagined about one shade after another, the whole being experienced at the pace of a medieval pilgrimage, with each figure schematically located in terms of related images and ideas). Then I thought of Whitman's cataloguing in his *Song of the Open Road*, in its way quite schematic as compared with the Williams experience, where now each step along the way is rather like the flashing of a traffic blinker, out almost as soon as it has gone on.

And here, as I have said, I would want to stress the strongly *dissociative* quality of the imagination's outpourings under these conditions. And the copiousness would be in the corresponding attitude, the ebullience of a poetic method that could find in anything and everything the makings of a poem, whatever might be the world into which, as Heidegger might say, man had been "thrown."

Out of such disjunction, new junctures would be formed. The total of his work (but I happen at the moment to be speaking of the whimsicality in his earlier works) is incessantly a set of gongs (gong, he hits this; gong, he hits that; gong, he hits the other) as one races on. We did not need him then in its incipient stages as much as we do now. The situation was already there, but only a shrewd wild man like him was responsive enough to size it up as he did (sizing it up not just in the sense of observationally saying what was what, but also more profoundly, in the sense of encompassing it from within, going to meet it halfway, thus *anticipating* our poetic needs).

Such is the basis of his work, and it charmingly invites us to relax, to let the lines happen. Then, every once in a while, something gets lingered on, for a whole development. Thus, out of the trafficlike hurry, out of the Vestibule State, and out of the tramplings, came things suddenly fixed.

I love to envision the whole man thus: the incessant bubbling forth, and the moments of clamping down. It's a good combination, toward vitality. I hope I haven't lost a page of his I once had, but things do vanish. The first line, clear as could be, is Pope's "Order is Heaven's First Law." The line is repeated six or seven times, and that's it. But each time, the writing becomes a bit more impatient—and the last time, it's just a squiggle. You also get something of his imagination if you reverse the order.

"The Forms of the Emotions...
the Pointed Trees"[1]

EMILY MITCHELL WALLACE

A Greek myth says that Orpheus sang so enchantingly that the trees uprooted themselves to follow him over hill and dale. When he stopped his music, the trees settled down into the earth again.

A likely story!

William Carlos Williams, I have no doubt, also charmed the trees, down to their very roots. In a wilder and more leisured era, he would have taught the trees to dance, as Orpheus did.

This month's *Harper's* reports various experiments that indicate that plants do have what we call feelings and affections, that the myth of Orpheus is not without some scientific support. Plants flourish when talked to, admired, touched. Derogatory thoughts may cause them to

---

1. William Carlos Williams, "Della Primavera Trasportata Al Morale," *The Collected Earlier Poems*, p. 64.

wither or die. They "love" classical music and are trauma-tized by acid rock.[2] Whether Williams knew of any of these experiments, a few of which were made in India as early as 1906, I do not know, but I am sure the discussions about a nervous system in plants would not have surprised him, for he was conscious, as he says in *A Novelette,* of "extraor-dinary recesses of the understanding still untouched by any generally practiced mode of approach—which artists have found accessible since the beginning of time."[3] Mrs. Wil-liams observed that "things would really grow for him."[4] However, since there is no record of an intelligible inter-view with plants that knew Dr. Williams, I should not speculate further about their attitude but concentrate in-stead on Williams's view of plants, specifically trees—and poems.

His poems without trees are inconceivable. The sky and clouds above and behind them, the flowers and grass be-neath them, the birds and squirrels and insects their inhabi-tants, lit by sun or moon, trees grew everywhere in his imagination, a signature of the changing of the weather and of the seasons, their shape an image of masculine energy, their blossoms a reminder of feminine beauty, source of new books of poems, their bare branches—as he says in "The Botticellian Trees"—[5] an alphabet, their leaves a song. His compliments range from calling them "the bastards," the way they "thrash and scream / guffaw and curse" in the wind and rain[6] to describing "the coral /

---

2. Peter Tompkins and Christopher Bird, "Love among the Cabbages: Sense and Sensibility in the Realm of Plants," *Harper's Magazine* (Novem-ber 1972), pp. 90–96.
3. *Imaginations,* p. 304.
4. *The Paris Review* (Summer–Fall 1964), p. 134.
5. *CEP,* p. 80.
6. "The Trees," *CEP,* p. 66.

peach trees" as "melting / the harsh air— / excellence / priceless beyond / all later / fruit!"[7]

Williams responded to trees with all of his senses. And when he saw a tree he liked, he might, if the owner and the law permitted, pick it up and carry it swiftly home in his car. His son, William Eric, in a splendid essay tells how

> the landscaping of . . . 9 Ridge Road was done with trees and shrubs pulled up from spots as widely separated as the Cedar Swamps out there in the Rutherford meadows, and the Mohawk trail between Greenfield and North Adams. Hemlocks from three different states separate the back and side yards. . . . There was always a wet newspaper or burlap-wrapped bundle of wild things in the car when he and mother returned from a trip. Ferns, moss, wild orchids, ginger, trillium, wild violets in variety, trailing arbutus, wild geraniums . . . . There was a daily ritual arm-in-arm circuit of the yard, usually early in the morning before leaving for the hospital, as he and mother inspected and planned the plantings. They shared a love of growing things . . . the garden was a major item of activity and conversation at our house.[8]

That trees were an early and significant, although "secret" influence, Williams acknowledged with pleasure.[9] Of course there were countless other influences of all kinds. To name just a few of the literary ones, he called Shakespeare "my grandfather,"[10] Keats "as familiar to me at one time as breath itself,"[11] Emily Dickinson "my patron saint,"[12] "Chaucer, Villon and Whitman . . . contemporaries of mind with whom I am constantly in touch,"[13] Ezra Pound "one of the most outstanding friendships,"[14] Wallace Ste-

---

7. "The Flowers Alone," *CEP*, p. 90.
8. William Eric Williams, "Cars."
9. *Autobiography*, p. 19.
10. "The Embodiment of Knowledge," Yale American Literature Collection.
11. *Autobiography*, p. 61.
12. *The Paris Review* (Summer–Fall 1964), p. 121.
13. *Selected Essays*, p. xvii.
14. "Interview with William Carlos Williams," *The Massachusetts Review* (Winter 1973), p. 135.

]22[

vens, another poet-friend "constantly in my thoughts."[15]
But of trees, he says in one poem, "The Avenue of Poplars":

> He who has kissed
> a leaf
>
> need look no further—[16]

and in "Della Primavera Trasportata al Morale":

> The soul, my God, shall rise up
> —a tree.[17]

In his childhood and early teens, Williams says in his *Autobiography*:

> It was an unconscious triumph all day long to just be able to get out of doors and into my personal wild world. . . . flowers and trees were my peculiar interest. To touch a tree, to climb it especially, but just to know the flowers was all I wanted.[18]

The first poem he wrote was not the one about the "black, black cloud" flying "over the sun,"[19] but a much earlier one called simply "Tree," which he did not recognize as a poem until many years later.

The original manuscript of "Tree" is in the Yale American Literature Collection. The childish printing on lines ruled in pencil is somewhat uncertain, with capitals appearing in odd places, but the drawing of a tree on the right of the page is very firm, with a well-drawn trunk and many leaves. Two girls stand under the tree; one child in a sailor blouse is pulling on a leafy branch, the other girl is watching.

15. *Autobiography*, p. xii.
16. *CEP*, p. 280.
17. *CEP*, p. 63.
18. *Autobiography*, p. 20.
19. *Autobiography*, p. 47, or *I Wanted to Write a Poem*, p. 4.

At the top of the composition before the title "Tree" is printed the stately, formal name of the budding artist, "By William Carlos Williams," not the "Billy" or "Willy" he was then called.

In 1927, over thirty years later, "Tree" was published in *The Dial,* a magazine that had Kenneth Burke and Marianne Moore among its editors. A "found poem" in the truest sense, not one word of "Tree" was changed for publication, though minor changes were made in the punctuation and the measuring of the lines. This is the poem as printed in *The Dial,* January 1927:

TREE

The tree is stiff, the branch
is arching, arching, arching
to the ground. Already its tip
reaches the hats of the passersby
children leap at it, hang on it—
bite on it. It is rotten, it
will be thick with blossoms in
the spring. Then it will break off
of its own weight or from the pulls
of the blossom seekers who will
ravish it. Freed of this disgrace
the tree will remain, stiffly upright.

"Tree," though not so fantastic as some of his later poems, is distinctively a Williams poem in its close observation of the silent drama of the tree's stiff dignity despite the rotten branch that persists in blooming. The child who wrote "Tree" could become a doctor as well as a poet, for he observes that the tree may cure itself, the branch break off of its own weight, or the surgery, the ravishment, may be performed by the passersby toward whom it arches its sick branch. The children not only leap at it and hang on it, but, a slight shock, "bite on it"! That is characteristic too; William Eric, his son, writes:

Facsimile of the holograph of "Tree" by William Carlos Williams, circa 1893. Reproduced by permission of the Yale American Literature Collection. Copyright © 1974 by Florence H. Williams.

William Carlos Williams. *Courtesy of New Directions Publishing Corp. Photograph by Irving Wellcome*

There were moments when we stood aghast at his temerity in tasting. A simple walk in the countryside became a laboratory session for the taste buds. We tasted the buds and twigs of the wild cherry, sassafras, birch and witch hazel. . . . We sampled the sap of the maple in spring and found it wanting. We hacked off and chewed the gum of the spruce. . . . Granted almost everything we tried was known to be the natural food of some bird or beast. But there were times when Dad alone did the sampling.[20]

In the time between Williams's first presentation of "Tree" and his realization that he was a poet, he dreamed of becoming a forester.[21] That seemed impractical to his parents, so he became a doctor instead, which was "lucky," he decided, "because it forced me to get used to people of all sorts, which was a fine thing for a writer or a potential writer."[22]

While he was in medical school he labored over his first *long* poem, an imitation of Keats's "Endymion." This poem went on and on and on, he remembered, "book followed book, poetically descriptive of nature, trees, for the most part, 'forests,' strange forests." The hero was a prince, lost in the woods, literally and figuratively, both a real forest and the "primeval forest" of the mind. Before the prince succeeds in his quest of finding his lost home and his own language, Williams gave up, he says in the *Autobiography,* "in disgust" with "heroics" and burned the poem.[23]

More years passed before Williams discovered, or, rather, recognized and repossessed his own language. But the gift, the genius, was there from the beginning. So much depends upon "luck and determination," as he says in the Preface to

20. William Eric Williams, "Food."
21. *Autobiography*, pp. 281–82.
22. "An Interview with William Carlos Williams," *The Massachusetts Review* (Winter 1973), p. 133.
23. *Autobiography*, p. 60.

his *Selected Essays,* a book he dedicated "To the memory of 'Uncle' Billy Abbott, the first English teacher who ever gave me an A." No wonder he wanted to give his *Autobiography* the title *Root, Branch & Flower,*[24] he who but for luck and determination might have been, in words from *Paterson:*

> a bud, forever green,
> tight-curled, upon the pavement, perfect
> in juice and substance but divorced, divorced
> from its fellows
> . . . .
> a green bud fallen upon the pavement its
> sweet breath suppressed
>
> (One, II, 28, 32)

No wonder he was so kind to other poets, stealing time from himself to write them letters and introductions. No wonder he listened so intently to the speech around him, the common language, seeking the poetry lost within it. And no wonder he continued to observe the trees, which had helped to teach and comfort him and which typified the long growth and complex preparation needed for a great blossoming.

As late as 1948, when he was sixty-five, he was writing to his publisher, James Laughlin, about a "secret book":

> No, I didn't write it. It's a wildly mushy romance . . . called The Sylvan Year. . . . A truly secret book that would knock'em cold if it could suddenly be put into their insane hands today and sweet! sweet as sugar. You wait and see for I tell you I refuse to let it out of my hands . . . . a 'beautiful' style—all in a forest in southern France, lost in the woods—adults lost in the woods! —like sweet children, but—Raoul is the hero. Yummy.[25]

I found the book[26] in a library and read it. Raoul is the hero,

---

24. *Selected Letters,* p. 295.
25. Unpublished letter, March 25, 1948.
26. Philip Gilbert Hamerton, *The Sylvan Year, Leaves from the Note Book of Raoul Dubois* (Boston, 1876).

yes. His last name is Dubois, of the woods, and he is the hero because he tells the story of the year he and his son spent wandering in a forest. (Williams must have noticed the similarity to his own lost prince.) Each chapter title of *The Sylvan Year* is a month of the year. For January the list of topics, skipping a lot of them, is: "Wintry Landscape —Mummy Plants—Common Teazle—The Great Mullein —Ferns and Grasses . . . Mountain Ash—Hazel—Structure of Trunks and Branches—Walnut—Oak—Ash—Poplar—Alder—Horse Chestnut." The descriptions are so precise that the book could serve as a botanical handbook. I expected a love story, a "beautiful" romance, and so it is, the daily record of an artist's love of trees and plants. Williams said he read the book when he felt "low." And he paid a larger tribute to it by expropriating from it, as great poets do, some passages for his own writing.

No matter how important trees were to Williams, and no matter how appealing his interest in them may be, one must acknowledge that a love of trees does not make a poet or a poem. In *A Novelette* is this short sentence, "Words on a par with trees." Williams's excitement about this statement, which he says is "so penetrant, so powerful, so inclusive of all good that . . . it will blast a million difficulties,"[27] made me ponder. "Words on a par with trees." The quality of ardent attentiveness that he gave to trees, given also to words, and to people, and to things other than trees, such as a city or a river or a red wheelbarrow—that does make a great poet, provided he has the genius to start with. "Words on a par with trees." Williams would never have agreed with Joyce Kilmer, even though he was also a New Jersey poet:

27. *Imaginations*, p. 294.

> I think that I shall never see
> A poem lovely as a tree.
>
> . . . .
>
> Poems are made by fools like me,
> But only God can make a tree.

Williams believed a poem can be lovely as a tree because what the poet does with words, which are as fascinating as trees, is "to make, out of the imagination, something not at all a copy of nature, but something quite different, a new thing, unlike any thing else in nature, a thing advanced and apart from it."[28] The trees in Williams's poems, like the trees who listened to Orpheus, have been transported to a new place, a different realm, made into a new thing.

Williams's insistent point, "No ideas but in things" may be thought of as pure Platonism or the medical doctor's *sine qua non* or the good poet's unintimidatable perception or all three. Plato, Williams learned as a boy,[29] says our love rises upward from the things we know to things of abstract

---

28. *Autobiography,* p. 241. Of course Williams did not argue that a new thing, poem or tree, *must* be "lovely," and in his parody of Kilmer's poem, the speaker is an earthy comedian, a malcontent who grumbles irreverently:

> Trees
> Of all the things that I could be
> I had to be a lousy tree,
>
> A tree that stands out in the street
> With little dogs around my feet.
>
> I'm nothing else but this, alas,
> A comfort station in the grass.
>
> I lift my leafy arms to pray,
> Get away, little doggie, get away!
>
> A nest of robins I must wear
> And what they do gets in my hair.
>
> Of all the things I had to be
> I had to be a goddam tree.

Previously unpublished. Poetry Collection, Lockwood Memorial Library, State University of New York at Buffalo.

29. *Autobiography,* p. 22; *I Wanted to Write a Poem,* p. 13; *Yes, Mrs. Williams,* p. 8.

perfection. The medical doctor bases his diagnosis, even more his prognosis, upon embodied evidence. A poet like Williams sees, for an example, some pointed trees. He observes them with Platonic love, a clinical eye, and Dionysian rapture, regarding at the same time and in a similar way the very process of observation, his emotions, his words, and the lines and sounds the words make. He may also be imagining the feelings of the trees and of the objects near them. From these multiplex relationships mysteriously comes a poem, a new form, a *made* thing. It can be filled with ideas, but the ideas come after the feelings and words, caught among the lines or hovering like a hummingbird above blossoms. "Nothing in the mind that was not first in the feelings"[30] is another way he described the process, or, one might say, no ideas but in things that touch the emotions:

> The forms
> of the emotions are crystalline,
> geometric-faceted. So we recognize
> only in the white heat of
> understanding, when a flame
> runs through the gap made
> by learning, the shapes of things—
> the ovoid sun, the pointed trees[31]

It is no whimsy of metaphor, then, that poems about himself as poet are also about trees, such as "The Wind Increases," in which he says that the poet's words "bite / their way / home—being actual / having the form / of motion / At each twigtip / new / upon the tortured / body of thought";[32] and "Portrait of the Author," in which "The birches are mad with green points / . . . . coldly the birch leaves are opening one by one" like poems;[33] and "The Pink

30. Unpublished letter.
31. "Della Primavera Trasportata Al Morale," *CEP*, p. 64.
32. *CEP*, p. 68.
33. *CEP*, p. 228.

Locust," in which the tree, also the poet, is "persistent . . . you will not easily get rid of it."[34] Even in a poem like "Lighthearted William," in which no tree appears, there is a joyful, wild, green feeling, a sylvan spirit:

> Lighthearted William twirled
> his November moustaches
> and, half dressed, looked
> from the bedroom window
> upon the spring weather.
>
> Heigh-ya! sighed he gaily
> leaning out to see
> up and down the street
> where a heavy sunlight
> lay beyond some blue shadows.
>
> Into the room he drew
> his head again and laughed
> to himself quietly
> twirling his green moustaches.[35]

---

34. *Journey to Love,* p. 24; *Pictures from Brueghel,* p. 140.
35. *CEP,* p. 226.

The People Who Use the William Carlos
Williams Collection at Yale[1]

NORMAN HOLMES PEARSON

Who are the people who use the William Carlos Williams Collection at Yale? I, certainly, am one of them. I needed just such a collection before any existed. I came to know Williams first when in the mid-1930s with William Rose Benét I was editing *The Oxford Anthology of American Literature*. In it, twentieth-century American poets (among them Williams) were first shown in academic circles as the equals of the anthologized giants of the nineteenth century. The anthology seemed brave; the recognition was certainly tardy. But perhaps the bravery was because I was only a graduate student, and Benét no academic at all. I met Williams through Horace Gregory when Williams gave a reading at Sarah Lawrence College. It was harder to meet his

1. The text has been prepared from notes used for an informal talk given at the "Symposium on William Carlos Williams" held at Fairleigh Dickinson University, in Rutherford, New Jersey, on Sunday, November 12, 1972.

writing, simply because no public collection of it existed. I did what I could to begin one.

Yale's opportunity really started with a human problem. Here is a letter Williams wrote to me on November 7, 1938:

> Dear Pearson,
>
> Living forever is an awful job, one wishes sometimes that one didn't have an immortal soul, writing would be so much more a pleasure. Now that I find it impossible to write, my mind is fast winding itself into knots of despair. This morning Floss and I in our agony started to clean a large boxlike semi-ornamental catchall that lies like a coffin across one end of our front hall. Books, magazines, pamphlets—a steadily mounting stream (and none of them so much as looked at)—pile up and are pushed under a lid against such a day as this one. What are we to do? Where shall we turn for relief? I don't know why. My own books dismay me. I wonder why I too have been so mad as to add to the horrible pile.
>
> One thing I can do. I can send you one of my new books of the collected poems. That will reduce the accumulation by at least one item.
>
> It must be change of life. It must be the weather. I go about forgetting to cork the cleaning fluid bottle. I strike my dwindling thighs against miraculously obstructing chairs. I pick up a book and dance with it vaguely, then lay it down again without having found a place for it. But that is only the surface. Inside I possess the heart of a fly, not even so much heart—for a fly will at least struggle against the spider. I hit the wrong keys. I am not even ashamed to speak of these things.
>
> Meanwhile four or five books must be written, at once. And I must help others who appeal to me for advice and assistance.

Williams began to send me, for Yale, odd copies of little magazines. There were few little magazines with which he had no connection, being a man of infinite "advice and assistance." I used to read the magazines before passing them on. Williams was educating me in what was happening, what was really happening outside of textbooks and classrooms.

I wrote him, "The bundle of little magazines arrived safely, and would be overwhelming if they were not spread around the floor of my study. I am keeping them at home for a few days until I can look at them quietly by myself before turning them over to the library. I have told the library however of your generosity. . . . I'm very serious in my own thanks. They make a marvelous addition to what we have. It works out this way. You sent along a run of *Hinterland* without the first number. I just bought from Weldon Kees a batch of little mags which included the missing number. Voila! You see how it goes." You see how it grew.

Other bundles arrived. Then in 1940 came a copy of his *Poems* (1909). It was Reid Howell's copy. He had printed the book. It was a presentation copy to Howell and signed by Howell for Yale. "So now," Williams wrote me, "if you want to give ten dollars to Dorothy Parker's fund for the rescue of Spanish children consider that I've given you my apostolic blessing—you've got it anyway." He was really blessing Yale's collection, for the gift was his and Howell's.

There was a war and I was overseas for most of it. To Charles Abbott, the remarkable librarian of the University of Buffalo and good friend to Williams and his wife, Williams turned over a large number of manuscripts and letters he had received from writers. Buffalo has a great collection. No one can study Williams in depth without going there. In recent years, Mrs. Williams has helped to build up a significant collection at the University of Pennsylvania, including his letters to her and the books he gave her.

Yale's collection is the most extensive. Its strength began in September 1953, when Williams wrote me:

Dear Norman,
    By now you no doubt received the copies of my books mailed to you this morning, by now I mean that sufficient time has probably elapsed for you to receive them. That has made me begin to think of disposing of more of my books and of my manuscripts also—for

]33[

whatever they might be worth. Some day, not now, but some day when you can perhaps spend a day in Rutherford we'll speak of all that. It isn't that I've gone back on my dear friend Charles Abbott but he has so much of my material that I'd like other friends, yourself prominent among them, to take a crack at it.

And so Yale bought what was not already at Buffalo, more than had gone there and whatever he was to write or receive in the years still to come.

The William Carlos Williams Collection at Yale has proved a magnet. It should be. Seven hundred books from his personal library reflect a part of his literary ambience. So do his manuscripts and the correspondence from the many writers he helped. Generous donors have added other groups of Williams papers. Edith Heal Berrien contributed all of the documents connected with her book, *I Wanted to Write a Poem*. Viola Baxter Jordan gave her letters from him, which run from 1909-46. John Thirlwall gave and bequeathed the material he had assembled for his various studies. David McDowell sent the original setting typescripts for the *Autobiography* and other books. There are Williams's letters to Dr. John Pearce, and many to Harry Roskolenko, Oscar Williams, and Louis Zukofsky. There are fifteen letters to Charles Henri Ford. Some fifty-five first editions came from me so that Yale's collection of his books could be complete.

Material relating to Williams is to be found in many other Yale archives. Some of those connected with Williams are: *Blues, The Dial, Furioso*, Marsden Hartley, *Hound & Horn*, Fred Millett, *New World Writing*, Gertrude Stein, Alfred Stieglitz, *The Tiger's Eye*, Carl Van Vechten, T. C. Wilson, and *Yale Poetry Review*. Now Yale has the Ezra Pound papers which, when they are available, will be an additional treasury, linking two old friends. Each of these groups defines the others, each is strengthened by their combinations. What helps to make a great collection is the collections that surround it.

Much remains unpublished in the Williams Collection. One is instructed by the unpublished and undated manuscript of "The Embodiment of Knowledge, The Beginnings of an American Education." "These are the Words," he says, written "To My Boys, Wishing Them Luck." "The fault of 'youth,' " Williams tells us, "lies . . . not in youth at all but with those to whom it has been asked to look: to its elders, the leaders, the professors who, when they are honest, acknowledge that they really know next to nothing at all."

We have hardly begun to know what there is to know about the writings of William Carlos Williams. Today, back again in Rutherford where I so often visited him, I remember another undated and apparently unpublished manuscript at Yale, this time a fragment, which he called "Rutherford and Me." "Poetry," he said in it, "is supposed to be written by carefree, footloose characters, wandering minstrels even though at times they may, like François Villon, have starved for it. I feel a little guilty because, unlike these poets of the past, if I am a poet at all, I have stayed pretty much— except for a year long jaunt to Europe—in one spot: Rutherford, New Jersey. That it is also Walt Whitman's state hasn't been much help."

He speaks of the bandstand and the trolley tracks, the weeping willows, and Turner's grocery store and Yearance's bakery. "I remember the cornucopias of penny candy I could buy for just one cent at Noden's and the tall old lady who sold it to me."

He tells of when his father first came to Rutherford from the West Indies. "That was in the day when our neighbor, old man Lillibridge, would take a camp-stool under his arm on his walks about town. When he got to a hill that was too much for him he'd open the stool and sit down to rest his weary bones. He lived to be nearly a hundred. You could do that in Rutherford in those days. . . ."

Then Williams canceled the last sentence. This was after all only a draft, and in the end he hardly went beyond saying, "The people to whom Rutherford has always been home have roots, traditions and memories which they cherish."[2]

A collection like that at Yale annotates "Rutherford and Me." It amplifies his roots, traditions, and memories, his life as a physician, his poems, his plays, his novels and short stories, his critical essays, and his letters from writers everywhere. A collection becomes a monument, but one which is always changing. Each person who goes to it goes for something new, some fresh angle, some renewed inspiration.

Who now comes to Yale to work on the Williams papers? Scholars from every state and from abroad, from Canada, England, New Zealand, Australia, France, Italy, and Poland. One is with us in Rutherford this afternoon from Hungary, Gyula Kodolanyi, who has translated Williams into Hungarian. "Rutherford and Me," because of the Williams Collection, increasingly becomes "Rutherford and Me and the World."

2. This and the previous quotation are from manuscripts by Williams in the Beinecke Rare Book and Manuscript Library and are © 1973 by Florence H. Williams and published with her permission and that of the Yale Library. The letter to me of Nov. 7, 1938, appeared in *Selected Letters,* © 1957 by William Carlos Williams and now quoted with the permission of Mrs. Williams. Similar permission has been given for quotation from other letters to me, © 1973 by Florence H. Williams.

Dr. William Carlos Williams, Poet and Humanist

A. M. SULLIVAN

My earliest recollection of Dr. William Carlos Williams and perhaps my most vivid picture of him was a long moment of silence as he stirred his tea, having squeezed an eighth of a lemon into the cup. We had been talking about his aversion to traditional rhetoric after our Sunday Morning broadcast over WOR in February of 1935. I had been impressed by his simple poetic statement addressed to a mop standing in the corner. Suddenly, he looked up and diverted the dialogue with "Look at that chemical reaction. The lemon has taken much of the color from the tea."

Williams's eyes and ears reported everything of sensory significance. He filled pages of notebooks with items from the trivial to the profound and recalled them as needed. Nothing was too small to record, not even the effect of lemon juice squeezed into a teacup. He sought the universal out of the particular and gave principal attention to the human

]37[

touch. Williams possessed a hungry mind that fed on people. He was an avid conversationalist with an audience of one or ten, but he was always the interlocutor if the audience was responsive, especially with the literate audience that he met in his home town. Occasionally he ran into a negative mind that sparked in opposition. One I recall was Dr. Oliver St. John Gogarty, the "Buck Mulligan" of James Joyce's *Ulysses*. Gogarty was a resident of nearby Wyckoff for a brief period following the settlement of a libel suit in Dublin, the aftermath of a comment in his autobiography *As I Was Coming Down Sackville Street*.

Gogarty and Williams had one thing in common. They could both write M.D. after their names. Beyond that there was little similarity to what their pens or voices might agree upon in public. They came together one evening at the home of Clayton and Kathleen Hoagland, a Rutherford gathering place for the culturally elite, but there was no entente cordiale between the physicians. After a brief exchange of opinions they were quite willing to "agree to disagree." Gogarty, the traditional lyric poet, and Williams, the irreverent iconoclast of the rulebook, retreated to separate corners with groups of listeners more amenable to their competitive egos.

The humanism of Dr. Williams became a major impulse in his epic adventure in the poem sequence of *Paterson,* a catch-all report of lifelong observations, enthusiasms, and indignations. Williams worshiped at his shrine in nature, the Passaic Falls with its drop of seventy feet. Here was the thing of beauty with its potential of service that inspired Alexander Hamilton in 1791 with the concept of "The Society of Useful Manufactures" in which Paterson became the prototype of the American industrial community. Here, too, was the design of the "Protestant ethic" of material success, the community of lathes and spindles driven by water power. Here was the vision of the self-sustaining city of skills with the competitive energy and moral stamina to lift the burdens of the citizen and raise the level of livelihood with social and cultural benefits.

A century later Williams saw the Hamilton concept realized, but with mixed results of success and misery. The poet of *Paterson* understood the validity of the hopes of Hamilton but also recognized that the city slum could be the price of progress in a mechanized society. As a humanist he realized the need for a readjustment of the power of the machine with the human impulse for equity.

This tension is mirrored in Williams's use of language, which is of time, place, and circumstance, and dramatized in the labor struggles of the Paterson Silk Strike and the city of Passaic's Textile troubles. He deals in the present tense with his passion for simple statement, and his rejection of Latinized English. Williams deliberately flattened sound values to emphasize an Americanized diction, a fact that is observed in his prose as well as his poems. Some critics modern and traditional have quarreled with Williams over his preference for the idiomatic phrase, and his desire for a simplified transatlantic English that is "American."

Williams was never remote from the daily chores of life. He borrowed experience from his neighbors and assimilated their problems as part of his own existence, whether in his career as a doctor bringing the first glimpse of light and life in to the hospital bed, or as a participant in the cultural events of the community. He was the humanist despite his temptation to test the ideas of political and economic prophets with whom he broke bread and sipped tea. He was a sampler of visions, most of which proved to be the rose windows of zealots. Just as the American writers of the 1840s were impressed as well as confused by Douglas, Ricardo, and Fourier, Williams spent conversational hours as a tea-taster of quality in dialogue. Most memorable to him were the talks with Ezra Pound, which began in the early 1900s during his years of intern training abroad. He was intrigued by Ezra's ex cathedra statements on poetry. They met on many occasions in France, Germany, and England when Ezra was weeding out the sacred traditions of verse craft from its deepest roots. Fifty years later Williams reviewed these talks in his autobiography and calls to mind his visits to Ezra in St. Elizabeth's hospital in Washington, where Pound was under duress for his support of the Fascist regime in Italy during World War II. He was troubled most as Ezra talked of his monetary panaceas, playing the same old cracked records over and over. Williams could only write sadly, "All I could do was to listen."

Williams recalled his own search for the cure-all of the Depression years, when the mercantile and banking systems were fraying at the seams, and the sudden deflation of market values brought forth a host of impromptu saviors with economic yeast bubbling in their veins. Many of these inspired voices were poets offering the variants of socialism, to which Williams gave a generous ear if not complete approval. He agreed that the critics of "the establishment" of the 1930s were entitled to their shadow in the sun, most of them expressing mild themes under new labels. None of the new ideas, however, echoed themes of the communes of the mid-nineteenth century, such as the "get-together" programs of Albert Brisbane, a New Jersey disciple of Fourier, or Ripley's Brook Colony in Massachusetts, but there were plenty of money and credit ideas to mend the errors of Wall Street and the bankers. The more formidable students and activists of Marx and Engels were getting together in cliques of the intelligentsia. Williams, as the humanist and liberal, parried them all, but he did have a personal affection for John Reed, whose body rests in the Kremlin. Williams visited Reed when the young rebel was jailed during the Paterson Silk Strike. Williams, who sought results in temporal value rather than tractarian preambles, actually supported the liberal platform of Al Smith during the 1928 Presidential campaign. Whatever violence Williams had in his veins was toward "the shape of the word." He gave "his passion to poetry," he tells us in his autobiography, and fought to cleanse the language of inherited rhetoric.

The Paterson of Williams's visions was a symbol rooted in history and folklore, but the city on the Passaic became a state of his incandescent mind, a universe of people compassionate and sensitive to life's values on one day and ribald and rebellious the next. The citizens of Paterson, always proud to have a poet of distinction as a neighbor, began to question their judgment as the sequence of the *Paterson* poems came from the press. The poetry took on distortions of photography with a strange delirium of captions. Something was being said in a mélange of words and rhythms, and they didn't know whether to protest or accept the compliment.

In reviewing several studies of Williams's poetry since the broadcasting venture of 1935, I was anxious to observe the changes in Williams's opinions of the generation lapse since 1935. I dug up a typed copy of the WOR dialogue. The fundamentals are still there but the scalpel of dissection continued to tear the anatomy of language apart. Whether Williams will make permanent impact on poetic forms or not, this much is obvious: he has stimulated and disturbed the grammarian sanctity with his rash treatment of poetic diction. There are dozens of doctoral dissertations in the works and several published books analyzing Williams's approach to literary communication. If Williams as a youth imitated John Keats with some facility, his imitators of the "shape of the word" in the Paterson sequence have found the facsimile quite difficult to approach or achieve.

During the 1935 broadcast, I opened the discussion with the question, "Can modern poetry abandon the tradition of costume language and rhetoric?" He was ready to pounce on the obvious before I could finish the question. He said, "Costume language and rhetoric taken as a term has a more or less distinct meaning in most minds. Something like hand-painted teacups. One doesn't ask modern painting to abandon painting on teacups. All one asks is that the limitations be realized. The difficulties and opportunities lie elsewhere, that is all. Most people find poetry today rather horrible, rather lacking in what they term poetry. But what they really admire is the past, and especially some rather soft, tripping, and gay thing that the past seems to mean to them. Or else some solid, logical, invaluable appearance of some master-work that no longer occurs today. And that to them *is,* by God, poetry."

I followed up with a loaded question, which Williams also jumped at. I asked, "Is the most successful of our American poetry rooted to the idiom of the language?" I had in mind the relative success or failure of Carl Sandburg who, in his book of poems "The People, Yes," may have strained the values of idiom by his use of slang; but Williams ignored the area of slang, and stayed with the term "American."

Williams, in a direct and specific reply, said, "There is no American poetry that is not rooted to the idiom of the language. There is other poetry written by Americans but most of it has been written in French. A little of it in Japanese, and some more in imitation English. But the success of a

]42[

poem that might be called "American" lies first in its identification with the sensual qualities of the language, which the poet hears in his ears all day long. If he ignores that, he has at once removed from his mind the only chance he will ever have for accurate statement, his last opportunity for subtle delineation of character and his major stimulus to musical pattern and so to poetic form. From earliest colonial times the English complained of our corrupt speech. What they failed to observe was that the words we often used as they used them applied to American, not English, objects."

I interrupted, "Can you name names and offer the specific instance?" His first example surprised me. "Certainly Poe was early recognized to be writing, not in English, but in the American tongue. Even Lanier, with his *Indian Burying Ground,* seemed far removed from any country church yard. Whitman is an example too obvious to insist upon. It is safe to say that it was the idiom which gave these men room for their development, as it was their failure to recognize the idiom that largely thwarted the Cambridge School, making them uniformly second rate. They thought American was funny. But they never realized how funny it would make them. When Emerson succeeded he seemed most un-English." His reference to Emerson was highly acceptable to our radio audience, judging by the mail response.

I came back to the shaping of words in our daily vocabulary, and gave some examples from Williams's own poetry of the vernacular, and asked if poets could abandon the "traditional" in rhetorical device. He tied up his observation to the sensory impact on the imagination, saying, "The ability to raise what is under the nose to our imagination is the difficult feat which poetry at least might reasonably be expected to perform. There is nothing at least to prevent us from using our daily vocabulary for this purpose if we find ourselves able to do so. This presents a different conception of poetry to the mind from that usually accepted. It is not usually accepted. If preconceived ideas stand in the way they had better be junked. 'Costume language and rhetoric' have largely been junked."

Gradually our dialogue swung around to speech rhythm, and the musical identification of a language. Williams never hesitated with this statement: "Poetry is largely music. If we persistently ignore the native music of our speech we shall end by being ignoramuses. We are not English in anything we do even though we use many words of English origin in our daily vocabulary. But we do not use them either in pace, inflection or sometimes even in meaning as any others but ourselves do. When language is packed, when its pace is quickened, when it is sharpened and driven in, it takes a rhythmic character. From time to time men have selected from this purely physical character of language certain elements which they have made into verse forms."

I picked up his theme here, and asked how the identity of American speech and poetry might be observed as time brought them closer together in structure and music. He hesitated on this answer for a quick mental review, then answered: "Different times and different countries have moved according to their local genius to build form to suit themselves. America may do the same. But these forms have distinct significances attached to them as of their times, the whole structure of the line and its various associations in groups is related to the general character of the age that gave it birth. As the understanding and the sensitivity to enlarged meanings has developed, poetic forms may keep reasonable pace. It might possibly come about that a new language like 'American' may find opportunities for invention today denied to others. New words and meanings require new contexts."

Dr. Williams had been greatly influenced by Thorstein Veblen, and the influence is reflected in his reply to my query, "Can the poetic forms of yesterday be used effectively in expressing modern poetic sensation?" His reply was a flat NO, and he continued, "They can be used—we still play the clavichord. It is very charming, too, but it lacks scope. It all harks back to the faulty conception of what poetry is inherent in the first question. A man should read Thorstein Veblen's *Theory of the Leisure Class,* before he attempts to go far in any phase of art. The value of old forms is revealed there to appertain too often to our vanity rather than our good sense. The major activity of any artist in any period must always be to discover in the idiom of his life about him, the life that his own eyes, ears, nose, mouth, fingers are seeing for the first and only time—to discover therein the lasting qualities of all art and to assert them in the terms he knows, the terms of his day of his own life. When he does this, he invents, he discovers. What he has found necessary under his living circumstances to invent, to forge, will be new, that is to say, unlike anything else that has been done before. It can't be otherwise if he has eyes and ears and a mind that changes."

Yes, indeed since the broadcast of February, 1935, William Carlos Williams went deeper into his well of sources for change, as comparison with his *Paterson* poems illustrates. In conclusion I would say there is something of the spirit of Walt Whitman in Dr. Williams. Whitman, who began writing gentle quatrains for New York papers, used the first name of "Walter" before he rebelled against tradition in poetry and rode Pegasus bareback as "Walt."

Williams in his aim for an "American" poetry has ridden roughshod, too, over the traditions to win acceptance of his gospel of humanism and "plain talk" in his poetry. How successful he may be depends upon the test of time. Rebels have usually failed to destroy traditional values, but they have always succeeded in rubbing off the accumulation of dust from the hard finish of the bone and beauty of poetry itself.

REFERENCES

Weaver, Mike. *William Carlos Williams, The American Background* (New York: Cambridge University Press, 1971).

Williams, William Carlos. *The Autobiography of William Carlos Williams* (New York: New Directions, 1951).

———. *James E. Breslin, An American Artist* (New York: Oxford University Press, 1965).

———. *Paterson* III, IV, and V (New York: New Directions, 1947–1951).

———. *Thomas R. Whitaker* (New York: Twayne Press, 1968).